5/12
10—
POET
PJL74

My Life
in
the Nineties

My Life
in
the Nineties

Lyn Hejinian

Shark Books
New York

Cover: Emilie Clark. "Untitled," 2001. Water
color, ink and graphite on paper. 30" x 22"

Shark Books is a project of Shark, A Journal
of Poetics and Art Writing

Shark Books
74 Varick Street #203
New York, NY 10013
shark@erols.com
www.sharkbooks.com

Also distributed by:

Small Press Distribution, Inc.
1341 Seventh Street
Berkeley, CA 84710
orders@spdbooks.org

ISBN: 0-9664871-9-2

I've never seen much that was typical   What? is the fiftieth year of my life now complete? such a living life? such an inconstant one? Imagine the film equivalent of this, one shot per sentence, the shot of this one of…. Then suddenly war broke through as I was typing something melodramatic involving an articulate, cognizant rose for money from the radio on the floor behind me, and my consciousness departed from its place between my eyes and hands. My head is against the scalding yellow wall, my toes have torn my socks, I eat something that's coming apart. I keep a light in case of tremor. I use a boarding pass to mark my place. As for we who love to be astonished, we close our eyes so as to remain for a little while longer within the realm of the imaginary, the mind, so as to avoid having to recognize our utter separateness from each other, a separateness that is instantly recognizable in your familiar face. Sure we are all in and as our times, but some are more in and as it than others. It both was and was not I who sat on the bed called America awaiting the television crew and preparing a monologue on science and the feminist of the West. I scroll, I paste, I feel the possible closeness and the impossible closeness, just as forty years ago I would feign nausea (so well that I did indeed get sick) so as to stay home from school, spending the long day in my room collaging photographs and pictures cut from magazines into scrapbooks, all of them together forming a sort of encyclopedia, with each scrapbook a volume of it. In realizing that much was left out, I discovered sentimentality — not the sentimentality of cheap romanticism but that which Sterne's *Tristram Shandy* (the Tristram of the infinitely prolonged conception) initiated and which postmodernism elaborated. No excuses. Larry's life, Paull's life, Anna's life. My friend's birthday was a day before mine and Iraqi musicians joined us at the Afghani restaurant in Paris to celebrate. I drove to an enormous Sears, its aisles trellised, latticed, grooved, and I walked around awkwardly with a pickaxe in my cart, looking for a small iron skillet and a bathmat and matching towels, maneuvering efficiently but with no sense of being seen nor even of being there, capacitated, in other words, anonymously. Short lines (of poetry) slow. Perhaps the immortal soul survives, but let's say without any of its experience and circumstances, released or detached, free of death and stripped of life — then, yes, autobiography is required. "What we term a long poem is, in fact, merely a succession of brief ones," Poe says. Little puffs of dust pop out from under the feet, emitting the odor of chamomile. The Atlantic expands (America departing from Europe) the same distance each year that our fingernails grow. Drifting science, the weather sounds. It involves in time meditation and out of time narration. The *Tractatus's* apparent terminus ("What one can't speak of one must pass over in silence") seemed as I considered it transitional, leading not to the silence of some transcendent, unutterable stability but to an other *extremis*, the present. She is 5, she is 25, she is 50 — the voluntariness of knowing that the life is mine must remain strong. The breasts themselves are a hunger to please. But here I can write it. So upright, twilit, quoted, Lenin was a person. Free to give or free to receive. The American press conceded. We were supposed to hate the war but love the warriors, to be unified at odds while getting even. Then my sister gave herself a middle name, a word versing the world — in fact she gave it to us all.

The familial given as a cookbook; the family gathered for dinner. This is a poetry of what is happening, nowhere disintegrating such decisions. And I went (for the last time) to the Soviet Union. It's hard to turn away from moving water and impossible to return to it. Across parallels the homeless move, only singly or in pairs, since they've yet to move in crowds. Across irritable, anxious, education cuts. A little boy playing on the street as we walked by suddenly ran at us and kicked the man who was with me, there was no misunderstanding, the humiliation was complete. The coaches shot him up with painkillers and cortisone to cover up the bone spur problem in his foot until the end of the season, when they kicked him out of school and rescinded his athletic scholarship. What had been Model School reverted to John Muir, what had been Leningrad was St. Petersburg again. One cannot be afraid to watch for such a long time that the uncanny is revealed — preliminaries consist of such eternities. Being a woman isn't a condition so much as it's a motivation, with momentum, occurring at various velocities and with diverse trajectories. It is clear that such a person as a writer, then, not only may but absolutely must appear in our society (but as what?). On Filbert Street, on Hillcrest Road, on Old Sudbury Road, Green Street, Aspinwall Avenue, on 21st Street, Treat Street, Shimmins Ridge, on Russell Street – the gestural, ritual, repetitive nature of every meal was comforting, though it might have been coercive as well, given our compelling memories — of tacos, mango juice, baked potatoes "buttered" with mayonnaise, and Caffeine Free Diet Coke (or CFDC), appearing like letters of the alphabet, of which none is superior to any other but which are chosen in accord with the word we want to spell. For every performer the present is more important than the past. I pause knowing that no one knows there I am. When I say "chapter" I mean "train station in Russia," that's what I mean by the word, and by "word" I mean "huntress" and she means "we should consider a day lost if we have not danced at least once." Self-improvement is not the same as personal efficacy, and altruism is not the same as agency. My husband was currently using a red soft toothbrush and my wife shaves her legs. Violence in fact almost never occurs randomly though that any particular instance of it happens just when and where it does may remain inexplicable. I said that I knew a man who, recognizing that his wife was undertaking far more of the housework, the shopping, the cooking, and the care of their child than he, calculated the discrepancy in hours and offered her an appropriate monthly salary. A groggy and possibly injured or only drunk man was sprawled just behind the driver of the bus in one of the seats facing the aisle wearing filthy pants that he was now wetting, the urine dripping to the floor, and I was embarrassed, implicated — just as years before, when I was in first grade, after my friend Loretta wet her pants in class and then remained as if caught in her own puddle, I hadn't wanted to go back to school, feeling that I had witnessed something there that I hadn't been meant to see and had thus prematurely acquired forbidden knowledge. But in every situation one anxiously anticipates the possibility that a political correction might be made. The place names in the 44th line of the poem hardly signify. The lack of plot and love of detail should organize my life not according to years or hours but according to spots and stops. Ships. The story seemed plausible, the situation seemed desperate — but then again, due to an emotional naivete that experience has been unable to shake, I'm inclined to be very gullible. But to remain passive is to engage in ethical mediocrity. Fervors put our thumbs on thistles. That's the point: the emotions provide us with conviction.

We need the language We have *to aid the senses* words to guard continents of fruits and organs. Knowledge is an incitement I turned over. I was in search of a better position, stranger strangers' times. From 10 to 1, dance one day and draw another; from 1 to 2 draw on the day you dance and write a letter the day after. My senses too seem to exist — I hear the sounds of a blue jay squawking between the leaves and suddenly again feel the many links between that and the minuscule elements of smell from the gray rain beginning to fall — but the well-known is not necessarily known at all. The moment of panorama, the momentum of preparation. Anticipation is not autonomous. In the dream I was accosted by a woman asking for a mouse with which to distract a great bear that was poised at her feet, growling ferociously, and she warned me not to run for it, she said there'd be no point, bears can travel at 40 miles an hour. Well (says someone), we still have the vitality of ourselves in boots from our days on a frontier which we made it our business to contemplate. Rising from behind in the morning, muttering, a phrase plays upon the conquering surface of things. She sang, "I drove my Daddy's Cadillac, from Dallas to the sea, but the prairie holds the cowboy, I'll always want to be." There is no best without its corresponding thing. The rest is discontinuous. The poetry is connection. We are players in a theater of struggling wills. Then write a letter *every* day, though you'll have no guarantee that the communicability of your feminity (or the fact that the substance and mode of your experience is communicability) will be admired – it's not you yourself but your life that deserves attention. Destiny must play a part in any good Western, suffusing the landscape with inevitability, itself an expanded frontier, and presenting the moral characters with unavoidable, and often unwelcome, choices. In the dusty town at the Plum Cute Beauty Shop they were offering "shampoos and other passive exercises." The body goes and the head seeks matter. This doesn't lack logic – it is a trick of love. The biggest tree is over there, the man said and pointed, reminding me of the contingency of my expectations. Not form and content but will and content. Just by being under the sky a person knows it exists (and has no need to explain it) — but at this I was interrupted by the smell of smoke, then rising flames, the vastness of which (as well as my inability, after having been told to pack the car to prepare for evacuation, to find anything that seemed worth taking, feeling instead abstracted, severed from both the material and the symbolic orders) subsequently and for many months afterward left me feeling insignificant, insubstantial, and abandoned. I gazed at the cadaver and held its heart, removed from a once melodious cavity. As dislocated as an angel seated on a cloud without ever having had to overcome the forces of gravity. They say that Goethe refused to let his life become "an unstructured and unintended sequence of events," but rather, "each major event in it, foreseen or not, was to be pondered and given its place in a newly interpreted whole." Then compelled to summon strength, to wake up, to get out of bed, and to accept captivity. It was late on Grand Avenue, after 1 a.m., the stoplights set only to blink yellow, the four lane street empty, and I was driving inattentively, until suddenly I was aware that from somewhere, some side street, a cop car had appeared and the guy was flashing his lights at me, flooding me with despair. But I am always shifting scale now. Out of blue rags comes a raging wind rough enough to make a rigid rain. Horses laboring to gallop in the sand, a banjo player in a restaurant moving from table to table. In such autobiographical writings we can trace the effects of mental operations to their source. There is no difference of truth that doesn't make a difference of fact somewhere. The skin moves attention from thing to thing. Emerald Ellie (as she was called, to distinguish her from Ellie Allen, the other Ellie in their "club") was "probably" killed by her boyfriend, Freddy J. (or Jay) Claybridge (a.k.a. "Garbage") and "certainly" by repeated hammer blows to the top of her head. The writer realizes her duty to keep the data of what's immediately moving moving. Facts not only are but they are known, and from the time I was old enough to know the facts, remember sounds, require sense, I thought such work had as much similarity to reality as one could provide. Toasting bread, waving the hose, lifting the cat from a chair, I gave myself credit for "joie de vivre." And we've known that — that changing of endlessness, since endlessness is right in front of us. Accuracy is not the voice of nature. The house was clean for its own sake, except for a scrap of paper that I'd missed no bigger than a speck on the floor, and I heaved myself out of the chair and picked up the scrap which, if I'd noticed it a few hours later after the cleanliness had settled, I'd have left. I am not saying that personal generosity will solve everything — it cannot even solve today, not with an act, not with anonymity. Perhaps it's the consummation of all we're going to sadden. The hill is gated, the light has bobbed and dropped, the dog howls, and a rat has torn the door off the oven. The West is confined to infinity. The "philosophical" (i.e., resigned) cattle turn their heads to look at us as we hike by and swarming from a small mound at the side of the road there are ants (they are social but do not pretend to come from any country). According to Tolstoi's Yardstick, humans get their ideas from words but horses get them from facts. I still, now and then, see Madame on the street, an elegant though tiny and now very old woman carrying a small bundle of groceries in a string bag, but I don't speak to her, out of shyness and the near certainty that she wouldn't remember me, whom she 'had' in her fifth grade French class almost forty years ago, but also out of terror, since she taught her class with such ferocity, expressing, I suppose, passionate belief in the rightness, the superiority, the perfection of *pied* over *foot*, and *mont* over *hill*, that she made my life miserable, until one evening, as I was riding to my grandparents' house in the little township in the Oakland hills called Piedmont, I felt the sudden triumphant pleasure that comes from linking one thing to another, the thrill of making sense. We live in a relative state, with prepositional sensations. At the live porn theater I was to see that each woman paradoxically hid her mound by shaving it. On a chair at night in old clothes at my desk beside the window looking out during a storm at the wind pouring over the trees under the streetlight. The schizophrenic, gazing at something, watches it turn not only unfamiliar but unreal, but the artistic gaze (and the resulting defamiliarization) heightens a thing's palpability, sees it turn not only unfamiliar but real. There is altruism in poetry. Come morning the wind in the sunlight is the color of spilling milk. But the hills are charred, houses lost, and the city stretches out, named for Bishop George Berkeley, in honor of his line, "Westward the course of empire takes its way." The knowledge is embodied — and the body is trembling, terrified, because it's unprepared, it forgot to get ready, it forgot to buy food, it forgot to dress. And so to believe it to be what we truly believe it to be we must open it. In words to have my moments twice, I writhe. It finds itself (or, more precisely, cannot find itself, and advances) staring at itself. The West is here — we can ground our uncertainties on nothing else.

We think of these,
the polar circles

I ask myself, "What's in a poem." These are places where the action never stops. The outside of the world — but this itself is that. Looking after, being ready before. Tendrils, I said, but my sister heard ten girls: ten girls in the ferns. Within those two weeks of summer, one in the Colorado mountains and one near the North Sea, I met three different women, each of them living by careful design far from cities and alone, and I took these meetings as an omen. Across in a kayak from Afognak to Kanatak with the mannish Mrs. Feather and the mannish Mrs. Farmer – every form of association is possible. The sentence is a logical form regardless of the matter. I remember even as a child realizing that pleasure lay in arranging it. A storm came in — blue-black clouds and wind — and I was excited by it, or by the anticipation of something else of which it was the gust. A shock, and I wanted to be as impersonal as it. I would take a solid seat and see. I would take the first four trees I came to, give them a day each, drawing them leaf by leaf, branch by branch, and even twig by twig as carefully as if they were rivers and the page an important map. The travelogue is not a foray into exoticism but an account of its author's most petty problems (and most banal achievements). It seemed that we had never begun and we would never be there. I imagined the austere inevitable stillness of the Arctic pole. Doing 'nothing' — nothing having no connection with anything, being a name without a referent, an unlinked phrase — it coincides only with itself, generating no surplus, no grounds for meaning something. It bears no relation to the marvel that is Hamlet's father's ghost, the body of a disembodied parent, who does indeed exist now even if only in the form of one who existed previously, so that one must speak of him now in a strange grammar, as one who exists some time ago, one now who exists then. I was embarrassed by the glare, or by my watering eyes, and as I looked at my friend her image weakened and the world closed in until I rose "in blind panic" overcome by claustrophobia from the swirling white table that had become indistinguishable from the sun. Horses pounce, no comma. Forget-me-nots his favorite flower: his rigors were always local. I was a year older now than my father had ever been, a year older, too, than the grandmother I "took after." It is we who are ominous; the future promises nothing. I studied the famous painting called "Sailors Rescue Women from Drowning" — in the foreground a woman floats, her face suffused by an ice-blue gray pallor, and behind her other women are being rescued by sailors who are in the ocean with them, while on shore other sailors are bathing rescued women, wiping the pallor from their faces, which are now round and healthy, though some residue of white remains around their ears like shaving cream. We know "tomorrow we will be here," and "every person has its double" to demand more logics from life. Reason looks for two and arranges it from there. And it wasn't so much hope-lessness as a sense of lessening obligation that made me think I too could die, dead before, dead after, but alive now as I say so. Northern stories always revolve around meetings with natural spirits and the problem of how to treat them well so as to receive their aid, while ours are filled with the boisterous dead, the restless guilty, implacable ghosts. And already in Cooper, especially in *The Pioneers*, American remorse serves to embold-en nostalgia, and human flamboy-ance is sheltered by the ghosts of trees. The river, clear and amber, like tea from peat, ran deep through the bear circle in the forest. Mineral always turns animal in the machines it symbolizes. Sometimes the will inspects the goodness of being and remains passive before it. In a socket of earth it burns. There are hunters there, all of them conservationists, and some tension develops because no one is sure who should take on the role of hostess to provide coherence to the occasion. Parataxis is characteristic of atheism as of polytheism, but while the parataxis of polytheism is limitless that of atheism is unbound. My students that spring didn't know how to talk in class, since what they could talk about — what they did — wasn't what one "studied" in schools — having the saturating experiences of music, shopping, "hanging," tv. They were having the subjectivity of consumers, lacking objectivity amid abundant objects. The grasses waggled, obvious ballads, dreams. An enormous man crashed through the drugstore's plate glass window, there was considerable commotion, but apart from a small cut on his arm on which the pharmacist put a dab of Neosporin and a bandaid, he wasn't hurt, the incident had been brought on entirely by allergies, he said, but they were "much" to his "embarrassment." Whatever the subject, the man said — feminism, thinking, individualism, sex, writing, science, etc. — sooner or later I perceive the inevitable approach of the topic with which Americans are most obsessed, that of their own violence. In one show, nature (the ocean) has polluted culture (the hero), he's contracted hepatitis from bacteria thriving in the surf around a supposedly unused sewage outlet that in fact has been spewing untreated effluent, the waves can be seen surging in the background as he says to the woman doctor who has come to warn him away from the beach, "When a big wave appears, I've always got to ride her." He was at Two Rivers and saw a woman standing on her head. The malice of earth? Its solace. Who are wanderers? Today's brightest spots are void, and indeed it seems as if I have to will all of all these days into memory, as if memory, which had a will of its own during childhood, was now reluctant to attend to the day, or as if the light accumulated by time was overpowering the details around us, the way sunlight blazing on a page obliterates the type. The sun has sealed the sea. I would write so I myself could see if what I'd written was right. An analysis of details alternates with scenes, and there are pauses for these analyses, themselves scenes. It is a work of moments inserted. And especially for love — because time entails inescapability. Along the border between fields of sunflowers turning, where only two years earlier guards had been posted to keep people in, now guards from the other side were posted to keep them out. We rowed out on the lake to the island in the midnight light, the water dark, cold, smooth, glowing. We stood on the deck in the Arctic looking north — a work of links and circles. We hiked through the pastel air over the tundra, mosquitoes leapt, lighter and lighter, more and more happy, on into the pale night at the edge of which the sun floated. Why not remember sleeps as well as dreams. Why not write with unbounded identity and geographical fluidity. Sentence by sentence, all these exertions (looping, jutting, and providing pleasure from numerous sources), these judgments and extensions, whose curves often repeat themselves, form a whole which, despite momentary pauses, is unbroken by the angles, shadows, and impeding particles included. But years are not pauses, not roses, and who, I asked, was the nation's President the year Herman Melville wrote *Moby-Dick*. I don't remember, someone says, but she means she does not know, she feels no gap haunted by the rhythm of a name she can't quite say, the want she feels isn't supplied with a name but instead is a wanting to know, so she looks it up, next time I'll remember, she vows, but a year later she didn't. There is no deeper secret to immortality than having lived.

And of these, the binding moments I stood long at the gate watching cows in tranquility. One by one in a heterogeneity, two by two in a plenitude. I stood at the window watching skateboarding boys propel themselves through the parking lot, up the makeshift plank ramp, and over three cardboard boxes placed end to end in a calm. We perceive nothing but relationships — perception itself is that. She was developing a rock garden in the woods, cultivating ferns, wildflowers, and miniature evergreens. My sleeps are the vivid confines of my mind. Little was left but the indentation. The road to Angkor Wat was mined. She hated to change rotations, to feel like a foreigner lost between wards. Vowing to alleviate suffering is not the same as anticipating a world without it. Early this morning I observed that after first light there's a second dark, and it's out of that second dark that the true light of day appears. The family gathered around the kava with continuity. I had wanted to be the doctor, but it had been the situation of the patient that most fascinated me, as if the one thing certain was the inadequacy of prior solutions and the one thing to be achieved was the reappraisal of possibility. My attorney lifts the tortilla from the burner, sprigs of mint garnish the platter. It's an oddity of U.S. law that a person cannot be required to incriminate him or herself verbally but may be required to do so physically (by appearing in a lineup, for example). The face of the cadaver was still intact and it had a pensive countenance. Immobility creates a profuse focal point, so that if we linger we blur. The pressure of the tongue must be firm, the release must be abrupt and clean cut, and worry as well will take some of the sense out. So we feel but do not see humanity. I eased the artery from the gray meat of the groin. I'll accept the risk that's incurred when one volunteers for doubt. While traveling (and we insist on motion) we shift the center of gravity and with it the nature of confinements. Then progress (according to the research clock) changes the look of things and with it the value of things. Love indeed conjectures love. Ships cleaving to the waves cleave the sea famously. Overhead inland a mosquito rings like a spinning belt. This is the year that culture is conjectured in Antwerp. Even this, said the man pointing to the stage — even this is a site of class struggle, embodied in competing linguistic nationalisms, and the result can be crazy and make organizing cultural events unpleasant, so we do it in English. Over and over the small research vessel climbed the north face of the 80 foot wave and fell to the valley south of it. A damp wind lashed the awning of the cafe, no shadows fell on the cobblestoned square. What is the nature of this strange work — but it has no nature, only condition. Dense, animate music, an encircling circle, secret, Magritte. I thought I saw a nurse in white aloft on a potato, but then I saw it was a swan eating a tomato. If it's metempsychotic it's Sisyphean. We would speak twice of what we see, we would agree and disagree. But for the Hopi (according to Benjamin Lee Whorf in "The Relation of Habitual Thought and Behavior to Language" which I'd read years before, had largely forgotten, and was now reading again), the word "day" has no plural form, since there has always only been one day, this one, departing with the dark and returning with the light, eternally collecting experience; "to the Hopi, for whom time is not a motion but a 'getting later' of everything that has ever been done, unvarying repetition is not wasted but accumulated." I see a large field of "carrots" — these are slender auburn animals resembling elk and they are browsing in the grass. A private investigator needs to be able to catch the telling phrase, as when the client's brother says he has "no regrets" about their childhood because "there wasn't anything wrong with it." He'd been the only man at the conference not carrying a gun, and while the others stood around the resort's swimming pool in the heat of the mid-afternoon sun with their "pieces" poorly concealed under their untucked shortsleeved shirts, he dove into the water and swam about, he "had the pool all to himself." There's a critical difference between calling the course "The Harlem Renaissance" and calling it "Reading the Harlem Renaissance" and for me the latter was the wiser course. I am compiling an assortment of scientific anecdotes, each one fill-ing about half a large sheet of gridded blue paper. Beginning from the body, a moving thing, we perceive. He felt he didn't "get anything" from high school but supposed the value of high school is that it "keeps you out of trouble." I like an answering voice at last light that says carry on, wagging the shadow of which you are the pre-monition. It's unlikely I'd attribute mal-ice to that. I found myself following Fall Creek and thinking up courses, skies without "sameness," perhaps something called "1899" in which we'd read Winston Churchill's *Richard Carvel,* Charles Chesnutt's *Wife of His Youth and Other Stories of the Color Line*, Edwin Markham's "Man with the Hoe," Elbert Hubbard's *Message to Garcia*, Paul Lawrence Dunbar's *Lyrics of the Hearthside*, Henry James's *The Awkward Age*, Kate Chopin's *The Awakening*, Jack London's "To Build a Fire," Booker T. Washington's *The Future of the American Negro*, William James's *Talks to Teachers on Psychology: and to Students on Some of Life's Ideals*, and Ambrose Bierce's *Fantastic Fables.* The artist doesn't paint clouds she paints time, she paints with the eye of enduring. The sentence, an island only temporarily and tentatively colonized, sails, an aphorism on a page painted by a stranger. This has little to do with immigration law, though there too there is a hero. We wade past (the minnows are ugly swollen things) and get on the boat. I am enraged — I think of jumping into the pool to fight — I want to punch the girl in the face. We were at the market but not at the one that was at 3000. He remembered a picnic at which the adults "were drinking" and his father had called his uncle "a fat slob," the uncle had told his father "to put your money where your mouth is," and the uncle challenged the father to a foot race, which the uncle "at 300 and some odd pounds" won. The warping of the floorboards under the kitchen linoleum must be the result of a long term leak, and I'd guess that the delightful women plumbers two years ago put the pipes in wrong. Who was the President that year? Some kind of consciousness is always going on. One begins as a student but becomes a friend of clouds. Please note that in my attempt to increase the accuracy of these sentences and the persistence and velocity with which they proceed, I'm pursuing change while trying to outrun the change that's pursuing me. Consciousness carries us farther and farther into the world. Perhaps will and fate are the same chance.

Intention provides the field for inquiry and improvisation the means for inquiring

Fences marginalize a cowboy. Let there be sentences — circular sentences; sentences incorporating pauses, roses. Life will add thickness ("the thickness of time"). It provides us with the potential for forming the relationship between our curious subjectivity and every fascinating thing. We are hurled to imagine ourselves hurling and we hurl together. One night I had the dream of "The Three Sisters and the Hangman's Hut" and another night I dreamed of "The Moral Trespasser and the Fair-minded Spring." Where are we? — "in a series," to quote Emerson, "of which we do not know the extremes." Shall we do some ungendering, shall we gently cross-dress. The fingers aren't stiff, but they weaken, forefinger especially feeling floppy, quivering, losing accuracy, distracted by a rhythm, like that of a train passing in the early morning hours blowing its whistle. There have been "developments," things are "dramatic." Despite a growing sensitivity to social life guiding my attention, I began to laugh — a slight revolt — for which I immediately apologized. In and as this. It's all just a worrying after the control that would get one to that perfect point at which it's all departure, all glimpsed, all discussed, our desire desiring itself at the moment that expectations are relaxed, in a quirky deepening of companionship, in the quirky depths of companionship. I walked a straight mile and then a crooked one to campus, passing from bright light into gloom and from gloom into bright light moodily but doggedly. Always when experimenting, one must be neither shy nor certain. Facticity consists in being at origin (speaking here not of the original how but of the original why) inexplicable (a fact has original inexplicability: that's a fact, bingo! no fact is flat). But we need the language to aid the senses, and it all begins wonderfully on page 82, first word. Every word is an experience in the genre of the gentle exchange. Once upon a time, far away and long ago, though not all that long ago, sometime after the world began but before you were born — I can't be more precise —

what do you think I am, a clock? Yes, events tend to cluster along the chronological line. I dream of a hero who is able to toss animals from a great distance. Permanent revolution, ongoing life. Our lachrymose dinner guest sighed again wiping tears from his eyes and continued to lament the death of the "noble poor bear," last survivor of the zoo in Sarajevo. But an imaginary world of vast possibility is an inadequate utopia, while an achieved utopia is an unacceptable possibility. To be born at all seems chancy, and having been born, that it should have happened now and here and in human form to me even more so, but after that the most remarkable things occur at points of forced encounter between facts of equal strangeness. I've done everything I'm supposed to do, washed my face, I plan my days, then I paid too close attention to the words on the page, noted the points at which, after offering only quick glimpses, they each departed from the ideas they were meant to convey, but the ideas themselves had already escaped me, and I thought I'd say all this (all that) to Larry, wondered at the desire to do so, the wisdom of the desire, the wonder of acting on desire, a life of reason in this deracinated condition, talking to people I'll never know better. A thousand thoughts and one thought. We must sleep for pressure, sleep for sprawl. The numerous ill lay laughing, several to a bed. The canny look on this occasion was an uncanny one, they saw from the site of secrets. On the sidewalk at the window outside the restaurant in the "ever-widening gap" between themselves and the rich stood a crowd. This is all familiar: Henry teases Jane, Jane intrigues Cassie, William shares Willa's enthusiasm for Charles Dickens. The poems (as you, curiously, didn't seem to have noticed) were on a variety of different kinds and sizes of paper, some on enormous index cards, some bound into sets of miniature books, some inscribed on maps, so it was not a manuscript but an exhibition, the meditation embodied by the work (or works) having been made exterior and public; the work was performance. The coward replaces a public dilemma (demanding intervention, objection, argument) with a private one (her cowardice). There were two of them suddenly on the ice, tails up and sauntering, paying us "no mind." I was on an empty road in an Italian town in front of a yellow villa, having come a long way in a black carriage to visit Flaubert. From here on the plot will involve a conflict between secrets and sequences. I was passing a church on a warm Tuesday morning as the organist (I assumed) was practicing or just testing the pipes in canyons of blue timber. She had "the greatest confidence in everything" which gave her a tendency to amiability, coherence, until she found that she had gotten along and gone along and now was "in a frenzy." My mother was singing in the ship's rigging. The waves were hurled apart. Later the Ranger confirmed that those were wolves. Am I willfully disinterested, you ask, am I complacent — no, I'm thoroughly pissed off. I "talk to myself" and *as* myself, too, not yet knowing what I myself (or, better, selves) will say, what the rules are and will become, first thought flowing in imitation of a previous thought of a previous self one could say with equal accuracy scrawling or sprawling without limit, and yet that's not right. On some other occasion, I may visit Cézanne! Let us thrill to the intellectual, moral, and aesthetic emotions. Visiting my mother's and stepfather's house in New Hampshire, I took great pleasure in seeking "great treasure" in the soil under the trees that had grown up in and around the site of a 100-year-old trash pit — shards of pottery, rusty springs and nails, old buttons, and occasionally unbroken bottles with long and narrow necks, though by far the bulk of what I turned up with my little trowel was broken glass. Meanwhile self-sufficient wild animals in great numbers (elk, eagles, bears, wolves, mosquitoes, midges, butterflies, deer, woodpeckers, etc.) live spread out to the north, each allo-cated to an environment appropriate to its needs, and each, adapting its belief to the evidence, sure that where it lives is "right." There are no unequal facts, I was beginning to say. They sat along three walls of the room, the middle of which was all windows, and I, their sole audience, sat facing into the light, blinded, unable to see their faces, so that I was forced to turn inward, to plunge into my role, at which they, my audience, gazed. It all lasted just about as long as a play, and then we went to a cafe, which is where I really learned something. We were not at the margin but on the border, mind lost in body, skirt over our head. Scheherazade told her instructive tales to the governor and after that he governed better. You should enthuse over that, not this. When one apologizes or fringes one's statements with disclaimers, one gives one's auditors power but also binds them to one — they are now responsible for one's shortcomings, burdened with one's inadequacies. The self is a site of time absorbing dissonances. I find that I don't really mind that the cheering at the outdoor concert escapes the site and can be heard for several miles around in the summer night. There is no simple organic link between two instants, instead one must make "a pathetic jump," passing from the first into the next, passing the power of the first to the second. But more of that another time. The writing moved sense and made it.

I could count to zero   Every word has a stak-
ing effect. What is the meaning hung from that suspend. Between during along including and all along. In the "Pedagogical" notebook under "Poetry and Ethics" in the section labeled "the limitless, the impasse, the border, chance," I find a notion credit- ed to Deleuze, who says all that ethics requires is that we not be unworthy of what happens to us. The narrative returns from a journey to the pole but the narrator is left behind. There's no stop, just rope and drift, loop and tug. I was listening to the ornithologically ambiguous sounds of horns, I masked my disappointment that we didn't pull over to look at the sea. I am no Robinson Crusoe. I wanted to

defend description, to elaborate on both the pleasure and the information to be found both in describing and in being described to, but the awareness, which came to me even as I was formulating my defense, that the third possibility, that of being described, I would hate, made me doubt my previous enthusiasm, though it occurred to me, too, that, though I wouldn't like to have people view me, see me, scrutinize me, I wouldn't for that reason condemn eyes, scrutiny, or sight. The head is at the hill where it so loves the view of the hill flowing on awhile. Here is the difference between objective and subjective, said Leslie Scalapino: one can make an objective statement about anything one can make a statement about; the subjective is that realm about which one can't say anything at all. One old woman coughs up a sapphire, the other blows an emerald from her nose. In war each side tries to convince its audience of the supreme value of what it stands to lose. Cast in Waterford crystal, the lifesize replica of Bear Bryant's hat sat under spotlights on a slowly turning pedestal throwing bright reflections out into the room while the fight song blared. They called it "swayt tay" and I left it in its sweating glass sitting on the table. It's the all-consuming consuming all. It is all about old boys and they are all about football. Around the periphery of the field, just outside the fence, runs a shallow ditch lined with hard plastic, into which, when ant collectors stir up the horses in the field until they are rearing and bucking and pawing and dashing about, the thunder of hooves drives thousands of ants. If one (being gullible, credulous) is to teach herself skepticism, she must resist the urge to provide explanations. The *non sequitur* is something (which does not follow), the *nihil sequitur* is nothing (which follows).

Things are all causes and their ever-changing interconnection is what we term destiny. Lightning danced over the Delta as we turned onto a muddy track and came in sight of the river flowing past an industrial site under a wide dark stone and steel bridge beneath which in deep shadow three white men sat in a rowboat fishing. It was with skepticism (more than irony) that I called the Mississippi mug that I bought at a shop just across the border my "freedom cup." I could call it fixation, embassy, convenience, or hyperbole. By negativity, I mean our interest in, even obsession with, the unknown, the meaningless, the unspeakable, the unapproachable, the unbearable, the impasse; by sublimity, I mean recognition of "the gap" and the ecstasy (with its concomitant sense of doubleness, sense of wonder, sense of awe, sense of alienation) that one feels in the face of the unspeakable; by affirmation, I mean a commitment to opening that gap in order to make room for new possibilities, multifaceted generosities, tolerance, the giving and receiving of pleasure. All the more costly (and yet, as we'll see, also all the more mostly). Doubt is a form of accusation, a putting under suspicion (since, if the subject is proven to be truly dubious, it will be discredited and condemned to irrelevance), but doubt in that case might serve as a release — leaving one to turn away, setting the issue aside with only one last shrug. And regrets? — regrets regard and some charge. One day the princess stepped across a stream, took up her binoculars, and spotted a flock of tiny birds, but the light was wrong and they flew away, and whether they were chicadees or bushtits she was never sure, although the word "no" had never meant anything to her. It is just as Hannah Arendt says, "Though history ultimately becomes the storybook of mankind, no one's life has an author." Mystics, Arkadii responded, have access to nothing through memory in flashes of their non-being. Yes. That there's the father of all waters, said the drunk man on the log, to which the sober man standing on the sand replied, then that must be the Mistersippi. Out in the country about an hour further south was the Sin Garden of a remorseful man. According to Goya, the sleep of reason brings forth monsters. It was my inclination, my desire, to be interested and thus to be pleased — to be "getting something out of" the situation — but instead of interest I felt horror. With the threat of death, the promise of death, there may come a sense of sudden freedom, but only for the dying, while for her friends and family her dying produces a sense of restriction, of limit, since, while the dying person will go onward, will "pass away," the living must remain behind, like prisoners. She tucked her pinky under her thumb and pointed her three middle fingers to the left to indicate that I was exaggerating. Large leashed lumpy dogs appeared one night in my dreams and they all pulled in different directions against these connections. The memory of that dream is now a mere abbreviation. I'm in a tent pitched on a slope looking West with my two cats, now as big as panthers, and a female lion, who has befriended us – or should I say 'taken our side' in 'another wild kingdom'? Who could argue that selves are pillars alone. Our souls are our copies, they ignore us completely. I interrupt, not to seize power (though, in a sense, I do so) but to participate, corroborate, collaborate. Of course it is pointless to say something that can't be understood, and yet, though you cannot understand my love for you, it is not pointless to tell you of it. Leaves are being blown through the open casement window, itself swinging, and with the leaves comes a moth, a sphinx. I pass from one genre to the next day, a seat of different sensations. There once was a beautiful princess whose favorite color was red and she lived in a dark forest where only the tiniest flowers grew and they were yellow. The molten metal cooled and was beaten into brittle rattles, while the little children prattled to the kitten and the rattlesnake battled with a turtle. Michael interrupted to say that his friend Ben considered vinyl far superior to CDs, and Rae cracked, "Hurray for crackle." Sleep receiver of words. In social stages we make our way adjusting to dreams at break of day disguising as fun our ineptitude as we're seized by untested solicitude. I looked closely at the photos of the faces of the frozen men, their lips drawn back, not to grimace or snarl but as if they were weeping. Waking phrases come unwanted, unwarranted: I am afraid not of their sound (though it's malignant) but of their banality, their illogicality. They are unfinished night thoughts, uncut sweeps, unchanted gears. Haphazard discernments. No. In what way. In this way. Life makes zero mandatory, life makes zero nearly impossible.

This is a hazard of happiness   This is happening. This is an homage to Flaubert. There was once a princess who was turned into a salmon and then turned out of it again. Words negate nothing — but this proposition is false, since if words negate nothing (i.e. don't negate), they cannot negate nothing (i.e., negate). A word to guard continents of fruits and organs. It is a writing of reasons. It is a politics, a chance. If we received our fate at birth, then the

57

question one would have to ask of a child is how will she behave while she awaits her fate. I am sent to Room 117, but I can't find it — I am told that it exists but it is in "the double world" to which my doppelganger has already departed, and, that being the case, I am already there. It was easy to pass between the barriers that had been set up — I just turned sideways and wiggled (everyone I passed averted their eyes). Animals seemed to have lost their fear, a wild rabbit approached, a hummingbird hovered nearby, the garden towhees had become familiars. Where there are borders there is barbarism. Then the gypsy's goose jumped onto the bed and pecked at my thighs until all the ants were gone. This created a clinical situation, turned for speculation. Under itself is the buried equator – but philosophers at a lake always think of going under. I would write nothing — the counting to zero, the stepping backward to the pole. Bug best because best belief becomes best. A run and if I broke it I'd have none. I stood at the xerox machine with a bandage under my eye hidden by my dark glasses ready to provide "on demand" an explanatory anecdote, pointless, why explain, baby, just say goodbye. The vultures swooped, flying so close that I could hear the fluttering of their feathers and the strange sound they uttered, more clack than call, a rattling like that of large seeds in a can. Fleeting charges of power, species, season, shape, race, location, gender. *Multum in parva* — a little russet pebble; *multum in nihilo* — that produces practitioners. And here is a woman in whom a second grade teacher discerned a talent for math. Service rushes seclusion, seclusion raises service. I pulled down the textbook on entomology. An actual thing does seem in some way to be the cause of this statement's being true.

But increasing signs of dreams have appeared — they have shuffled forward, following the woman in the still bulk of her chair to whom so many pauses occur that she must count continually forward and then back or else she'll be surpassed. The speakers would shift, giving way to speakers within and to speakers within that. Fate never fails. Now almost 100, the old woman, in her near total deafness, was able nonetheless to greet and exchange extensive pleasantries with all her visitors, knowing from long habit a full stock of phrases and where they should fall and prepared also with compliments such as "it's lovely to see you" or "how nice you look," which might fall anywhere. Their smiles stretched wearily across her face. I buried the blameless bundle of hair. I lovingly took the head in my lap but it lay upside down and looked like that of a cyclops with an *ocula dentata*. We know people by what they do, yes, but also by what happens to them. A cowboy will want to be known as that as he waves his hat to think a real individual is created in visibility. Response: aphorisms are fatuous. I blurted out the secret and gazed at the ghost of having told it. Having been told by my sister that my nephew wants to get his college degree in history, I spoke to him with an enthusiasm I knew to be "contagious" of the infinite re-(or pro-?) gression that constitutes the interpretations we call "history," interpretations which themselves each have a history, which in turn — but No! he interrupted, don't tell me that! throughout my entire childhood I've been *terrified* of infinity! and that's why I've always wanted to study history — it's limited, to the past! so don't start telling me the past is infinite! That forest with the creek falling through it now has the status of a state park and the old ghost town at the end of the five mile trail that of an abandoned museum. I could fill notebooks with things interpreted differently, I could puke. No, we were not sinking. The sea is hard. We are warned against the thorns of the compass and the sun so we are prepared. Hightailing it toward the sunset with the sun in my eyes I came all over goosebumps. I found the birds ominous, but the omen was good. We stay in and on the evidence. I'd been sure that the talk, no matter the degree of animation, no matter the force of our agreements or disagreements, was all intended for the general good. But it's been hot, or rather the weather has intensified, becoming concentrated, so that people sweat as if sensing peril. The strangers participate in events, some of which last no more than a second and some of which have been unfolding for years. A pause, a glance, a rose, a knitted hat, the passing by of a passerby: something on paper.

They had been bigots, they had called my father Pinko. A turbulent dispersion of ink in water drawn by fountains to the inside of my world. It is hard to turn away from moving water, the beneficial bonfire in which you burned the clothes. Creating meaningfulness for the meanings this conveys is its meaningfulness. The whole barnyard. Your Willie to my Winnie was so convincing that alarmed nurses rushed in. I thought I saw a crumpled blanket lying on the bed, but then I saw it was an improviser standing on his head. What lives in the grave are bones and reputation, what dies is experience. This happened in the blink of an eye, but ever after the princess remembered the river — its dappled shadows, the weaving of currents of warm water through the cold, the slowly tumbling rocks in the rills over the shallows. All of it, if you've got the time.

Along comes something, launched in context That's an affirmative. And yet we have the pessimism to crave. Article adjective adjective noun verb preposition pronoun noun comma pronoun noun dash gerund copula preposition article noun. Now compare that sentence of last night to this morning's sentence addressed to you, in and out of the house and I can't decide about the movie either, but really I think it would depress me — the color, the plot, the end. For a spider to move from the center of the web toward a stimulus in the web, the spider needs conviction. Anaximander observes (or so Karl Jaspers says), that "once the world has come into being, guilt is no doubt an inevitable consequence of its antagonisms." Reason looks for three. Can this counter corporation. The explorers moved in the course of empire, the horizon widened what it cost them. Kings playing chess on fine green sand. But — though, strictly speaking, observation cannot demonstrate this, since, though they are, they can only (though they must) be supposed — large parts of the day refuse to come forward, and, if they deposit themselves anywhere at all, it is certainly not in our minds, we are dispossessed of them, and they will never belong to us. I wake with emotion, but what if the emotions are not 'triggered,' what if they are not responses but capable of rising independently, as pure affect. A human, too, is a "thing in itself" to itself. Character, stray convenience, the laugh, the catch. The focus of one's work may lie somewhere other than where one thinks one is focusing. It seems from our methodical and even obsessive habits of attention, though they are far inferior to those of the patient and meticulous empiricists who year after year first measured the course and ever-changing relative position of the stars, that we continue to maintain a belief that the advance of the hour or day (or, for some, even of the year) entails its coming to mind and that the aggregate, the accumulation of arrivals in consciousness (like that of fruit flies to a rotting peach) will add up to our knowing, at the very least, just what our life has consisted of. Obscure. As Gertrude Stein's one time mentor William James observed, this is "where things happen": "reality, life, experience, concreteness, immediacy, use what word you will, exceeds our logic, overflows and surrounds it... — and by reality here I mean where things *happen*." If then whenever nonetheless worldly — because worldly. The photographer is depicted as a young man hurling thunderbolts in the bards' circle, the cluster of cows couched in the dew at dawn strikes a dolorous chord, and the shoemaker, having suffered a heart attack, closes his shop. One wants one's work to be shareable — one seeks the shareable (*not* the universal). The entomologist, as she herself says, can tell you everything she knows about ants but nothing as to what ants know about themselves. It's a space of appearance, a space of dilemma. Parallelisms — one has to follow one's parallelisms. The deep blue paint around the doors of the house is meant to ward off evil, and if it can't do it all, the statue of the Virgin of Guadalupe is meant to do the rest. Two stunning men dressed in black and wearing brown vests whom I took to be gypsies were singing and playing their guitars at the Spring Street station, twins who were, as far as I could see, absolutely identical, except that one was a tenor and the other a baritone, their two voices playing off each other brilliantly, and I let several trains go by, which is why I was late. An event is an adventure of the moment. A man a woman arrives from the East the West bringing taking a summons dismissal that I am sending following and my confusion is clear unclear. The apples rotting in the grass below scented the dust which two hovering bees very slightly stirred before darting off as I descended. Intention provides the field for inquiry, improvisation is the mode of inquiring. You can see where a coyote crossed a tile. All that occurs does so in many ways. But bigotry is almost always devoted to enforcing separation and sustaining separateness. Flash's party discovers that Ming's scientist has perfected death dust so that it will only kill people of high intelligence. Doubt seizes — it grasps at the very things it doubts. I'm an internationalist then, i.e., an antinationalist — yes. When confronted with the challenge of judging the ethicality of another person's actions, it is best to assume that the situation in which they occurred was complicated. Things, being perceived, produce my reasons. There are an infinite number of sequences underway. My grandmother vowed to learn a new word every day and never at this age be ashamed to dance. The secret, she said, was in the pomegranate seeds lacing the salad with aphrodisia. Some of the lines in this family saga must be inscribed in Spanish. Here's a "situation" for a novel: a passionate woman finds herself so humiliated by the effects of age that she can hardly bear to go out, she feels disgraced, she is appropriate to no situation, she decides to found a theater company. This sign of art, this single indication, is marking a site at which at some other time some other human lived and thought. Two years later I will rise early and patiently await the changing state of my being complicitous with my fate. Hold this position for a part of a second, then release the pressure quickly by removing the tongue from the gums, deftly. The realm of the incoherent yields a profusion of fruits. The novel will conjure up a family I never had. I remember that I sat in the apple tree and ate a Gravenstein, still cool with life from the tree in the hot summer afternoon sun. It would be like this one, replete with unfathomable discrepancies. Three eggs and a corn tortilla — imaginary objects. Then the feral cats that Senora Paz feeds nextdoor come over the wall at night and shit at her feet. There's only one antidote to the dust — polarite. It is inaccurate to say that he who cannot love turns up frequently but remains unloved. Who we are — it is only partly revealed in the patterns of our lives — something remains hidden in our intentions. We take the great parts of a human life to be distinct, far more so than the transitions that oppose and distinguish them, but childhood and adulthood, youth and age, are never juxtaposed, unless perhaps in spaces like those that lie between the frames of a film — and it was in just such a space that the dancing at the wedding began. For experimentation here augment, insert, extend. The members of the mariachi band, somber as always, were waiting just outside the mission doors. One must sustain the value of the real world — it must be valued — when it is devalued it ceases to compel recognition. There has always only been one day, and with it we are developing a lifelong relationship.

Meaning reasons sentenced haply From the first moment I saw this I wanted to write on it. And strange as it may seem, the resulting story interests me not because it proceeds toward an end but because what proceeds works backward toward a beginning and begins. I'm *still* an existentialist. "Existence precedes essence": we make our appearance and then define ourselves. Existing never to non-exist again. We knew he'd be a boy, and we rocked in anticipation, waiting for him to figure out. Even as an infant, he broods bravely. Listening to the wind in the trees I heard sounds which seemed to have had their origins, if not in another galaxy then at least in the idea of other galaxies whose remoteness was not just geophysical or astronomical but emotional, and I wanted to know more of it — I lifted my head off the pillow against which my ear had been muffled and opened my eyes. Augustine notes this moment and says, "I have become a question to myself." It's a lyric shuttle or a carpenter's kettle, and we can make it mutable. The real are the active ingredients of a metamorphosis. Here is a thought, no longer mine, and I called it *amor fati*. The politician binds his thinking to results; the poet must renounce results and continue thinking. But real referring is worthy of respect. It used to be that one referred to "so-called language writing," but it's time to omit the "so-called" (or to regard it as a so-called "so-called"). Meanings are nothing but a flow of contexts — names trimmed with colored ribbons. But those who favor the material, contingent, or a *posteriori* features of the world are generally labeled empiricists. The world is what I'm made of, but the world is not made of me — it was already there, it will be there afterward, what is it. Too many questions. Perhaps one records one's moods ("June 26: gloomy, irritable — as if grieving" or "July 5: excited, restless — distracted by potential happiness (but perhaps happiness and potentiality are the same thing?)") not out of narcissism but in the hope that they may prove a register, indicative not only of the state of one's psyche but also of the state of the world. This moment exists in two temporalities, it exists always and briefly. It is time itself, particularly since the shift from a product to a service economy, that is being asked to yield increasing amounts of wealth. Many times upon a time there lived a bird who laid a figure on a twisted bough and invited a spider to help her raise it. They called the great rock Aphrodite. A single African flower appeared on my father's grave — unanticipated but not by chance. A windmill doesn't come to a location however but rather a location comes into existence because of a windmill perhaps a bridge. But what of the trapper adopted by the Pomo and given the name of Never Mind. The being at a loss. At the site of the pass into the postmodern infinity called the border I sat intransigently, laughing. He needed only hot water, as he had his own tea. If I were to decide to insert into this book — as much an exhibition of reappearances as an autobiography, since the self it "expresses," existing only in and as writing, and with that writing broken into sentences, changes place and even disappears behind the familiar — photographs, they might impede or even arrest the "developments" on which the meaningfulness (the acknowledging of the familiar's reappearances) depends. Others want to go into the basement but that doesn't seem logical – why would the basement be safer. As we were walking on the beach we were joined by a shorthaired mottled brown male dog who seemed to feel fond of us, looking back if it got ahead to make certain we were following or running to catch up with us if it fell behind, and then suddenly it left us. As William James says, "The idea of chance is, at bottom, exactly the same thing as the idea of gift.... [a] name for anything on which we have no effective *claim*." Commas between the penultimate and ultimate of a series, question mark mid-sentence, yes, but let tone determine emphasis, and let tone determine query at sentence's end. There are ironies between aphorisms — traces of sensibility. I was "seething" with irritation, and the irritant was myself, or, rather, the irritation, since what had provoked it (a mess and the picking up that eliminated it, carried out in a kind of hurry, even frenzy, brooking no interruption, no pause, as if it had to be carried out against a deadline) was gone, and I wondered what had caused the initial sense of hurry, since, though I recognized that the cleaning up of the mess (unwashed dishes, sections of the newspaper strewn on the table and couch, petals on the bookshelf from a vase of no longer fresh delphiniums, laundry needing to be folded and put away, etc.) was all a preparation, what I was preparing for was not some inspection, the arrival of guests, some point at which I had an appointment, etc., I was preparing instead for preparedness itself — that being in readiness, which is, in fact, an end in itself, because it provides so much pleasure. My father returned to me in a dream in which he turned to me (I was passing an enormous store, he was standing at the window within, he passed like a ghost through the plate glass, and I introduced him to Larry). There is continuity in incompleteness. I perceive, I interfere — with details repeated and themes dispersed. Wide awake, sipping now and then from a cup of coffee in a saucerless blue and white cup now half gone and half cold beside me, I think that to write is to refigure, though refiguration is likewise the work of dreams. The night is never neutral to us. The obvious analogy is with music. We plan an evening out for our evening off and opt to stay in. I feel the same old ambivalence, concede as before and as usual hasten home, none of this being new to me. Reality extends into the realm of the apparent and you must consider it. It was eight years ago, in the metaphorical period before the literal Desert Storm that I first heard (from George Lakoff) the term "electronic mail," but it wasn't until five years later, when, thanks to Jalal Toufic I encountered the notion of "the differend" that I could begin to discern the extent of the problem with it. Still, the latitudes don't change their order though spinning the many birds migrating within their solitudes. Philip has remained sardonic but he has become less discontent, Amanda has weathered menopause but has little advice to offer Kate, who remains disdainful, for her part, of Julian's continuing noble hypocrisy, Gil is out of seclusion and playing the violin, Carol has lost weight and Florence has gained it, Dmitri scowls and now speaks seven languages whereas Ralph only speaks local idiolects, and Petra speaks too often and too loudly of her son, but we all lose credibility for awhile now and then. One is not apt to write down trivial anecdotes about merely casual friends. But one can feel the effect of capitalism's increasing control over time, the incremental process of the life being lost. We'd been on side roads for a couple of hours when we pulled into a dirt parking lot outside a small road-side cafe at whose counter a cluster of locals was loudly discussing the blow job. We'd been through sheep fields and confessed, and after we'd dipped our boots in the sink and run knife and fork over their soles, we were shown a confiscated shark penis, a desiccated baboon head, an array of hooves from deer and antelope, and five cans of British beef soup. Sleep says nothing — it has made its break. The dog joined in and tore off the whole of the man's face while the man, his arms clasping it, broke every bone in the dog's body, and there the pair of them lay, near death, each having seized what seemed to be its only chance. Other combinations make sense, too: sentence reasons meaning and meaning sentences reason. "Sentences must stir in a book like leaves in a forest," said Flaubert, "each distinct from each despite their resemblance." Our borders provide us with a theater for exaggeration. Nothing and happily. It is the task of art to preserve disappearance.

Now long past　　　Again.
beginning, as a　　　Afloat,
longterm beginner, I begin　　alone,

abruptly along. Annoyed. The begin-
ning photographer falls upon objects.
She evinces concern for the cognitive
state of the poet. It has proved
impossible to circumscribe my enthu-
siasm, I have been curious to learn
other people's opinions and I have
never been able to remain indifferent
to them. Whenever I have an emotion
(a sense of affirmation (or, in the
broadest sense, love), or fear, frustra-
tion, or anger) it means for sure that
something is "at stake," there is mat-
tering. Poetry and aboutness and
acknowledgement and barbarism
and border. Where as a child I used to
be afraid of lockjaw with its resem-
blance to stubbornness, later I feared
the madness that filled the gap
between what I meant to say and
what I did say as it widened. Fins to

ears, scales to skin — the harbor bore bees. And now to know the California sisters, painted ladies, monarchs and admirals. One should put one's mind, if to anything, then to one's life (according to Socrates). I attribute to myself what has happened to others, as when, after speculating that it must have been because of a spider bite that my right elbow had become hideously swollen, developing a protuberance the size of a tennis ball, and describing it months later to a friend, suddenly I remembered that it hadn't been my elbow at all that had been affected but L's — and, while I can claim that this propensity is the product of a vivid imagination, it wasn't compassion that had led me to claim that injured elbow for my own but a kind of possessiveness over experience, a greed for experience. We don't begin from a nonchalant blank, beginning is a barrier to that. I'm now armed with a blade but it has to be tempered. I went to see "The Western Mania for Collecting the World," a film. The tenor sang, "In time of war, no one should think of himself," and the soprano threw her spoon down in disgust. Schopenhauer, they say, was a frequent guest because he loved sausage and knowing that he was feared by "the poetical regulars." Pilar? — Johanna? — Dora? My character can proceed without any more name than that of a beginner. Finn. Marka. Window is the name for that which is limited neither to entrance nor exit — and why? — well, because one can smudge it, it is *something.* The sun is in such torrents that I don't go out. It's community, i.e., force of character. There is a future. She'll begin life in the golden house with cobalt trim in Coyoacan whose garden wall cannot keep out the prowling cats kept by the widow Paz. It is true that life springs only from continuity and equally true that it springs only from discontinuity. My mother said I look at what will follow me and am content. Death, destruction, deduction, Dégas, Delacroix, delayed coherence. For one hour each day I will view the world as raw material for my inspiration, my arbitrariness, my needs. Fifteen stamps, not yet designed, will emblemize the decade and bring the century set to its conclusion. The figure I remember will be living a different life from this, not at the beginning and not at the end — those we will share — but now, in the time between. Once each day dysphoria suffuses her, a palm, a seive, a hollow. Decipher decision. The old writer is neither serene nor exhausted. Those who show disdain for being understood are not the writers of difficult works but the owners of moment. The women sold what they'd sewed and the men in the mines struck. She told me that morale was low, the pace frenzied, there were better jobs she could get, so she had decided to quit her job, but she "couldn't say no," her dismay (fear? guilt?) at "casting negativity into anybody's way" was so extreme that she postponed meeting with her boss week after week, and she works there still. In the gaps between what you want to do, what you think you are doing, and what you do, what exists but you wanted to suppress finds a way in. The water is the spider. And if the full span of the wind filled sail that we call our attention were allowed to spread, then the shadow it would cast would so darken the currents into which we drive as to render them impenetrable, before and behind as below. Afloat sometimes people hold rocks afloat. The woman who had stumbled at the curb entered the restaurant and once seated she began to cast dice, pitting her left hand against her right. I would rather settle for translations than have all poetry occur in some global poetic language. Behind her the Armenians were playing backgammon. Never use white except for that which the paper provides. There is an as effect. We know people by the things which cause them to change. Through the snow I walked and followed in fading footsteps. I agreed to trade my seat with that of the wife of the man assigned to the seat beside me and moved back two rows to what had been the wife's seat, a middle seat into which I was climbing so as to wedge myself there between a heavy man and a woman with a baby, when I caught the eye of a woman seated across the aisle who smiled and commented, "No good deed goes unpunished." Such displacements alter illusions — which is all to the good. My daughter's two turkeys have been set to rest by her chickens. The hummingbirds in my son's garden are still beset by feral cats that come over the wall from the garden of the poet's widow, but the two eagles that have recently appeared in the highest branches of the cypress tree over-looking the neighborhood appear not to be watching with disinterest. There is a vast field in which to practice for anyone wishing to acquire solid knowledge of what matters. Each film is 10 inches high and 22 inches long and if I could show one it would last 6.6666666 etc. seconds, i.e. forever. The old woman "seeks solitude," her mind "is elsewhere," she "loves to roam in the woods," she "has visions," and she "sings in her sleep." We are not forgetting the patience of the mad, their love of detail (a cellist in a tree with a microscope and a badg-er in bed with a book, etc.) — every-one is out of place in a comedy. One must eliminate fear in order to create a space for living an ethical life. Subjectivity at night must survive hours during which it encounters nothing that is conscious of it and have nothing to judge but itself.